SATURN

PLANETS IN OUR SOLAR SYSTEM

CHILDREN'S ASTRONOMY EDITION

SPEEDY
PUBLISHING

Speedy Publishing LLC
40 E. Main St. #1156
Newark, DE 19711
www.speedypublishing.com

Saturn is the sixth
planet from the Sun.

Saturn is the second-largest planet in the Solar System with an average radius about nine times that of Earth.

Saturn is the
lightest planet.

Saturn is named
after the
Roman god of
agriculture.
He was called
Cronus by
the Greeks.

If there was a bathtub
big enough to hold
Saturn, it would
float in the water!

Saturn has a
small rocky
core covered
with liquid
gas that is
composed
of hydrogen
and helium.

Saturn has a hot
interior, reaching
11,700 °C at its core.

Saturn has a ring system that consists of nine continuous main rings and three discontinuous arcs and that is composed mostly of ice particles.

Saturn is the flattest planet.

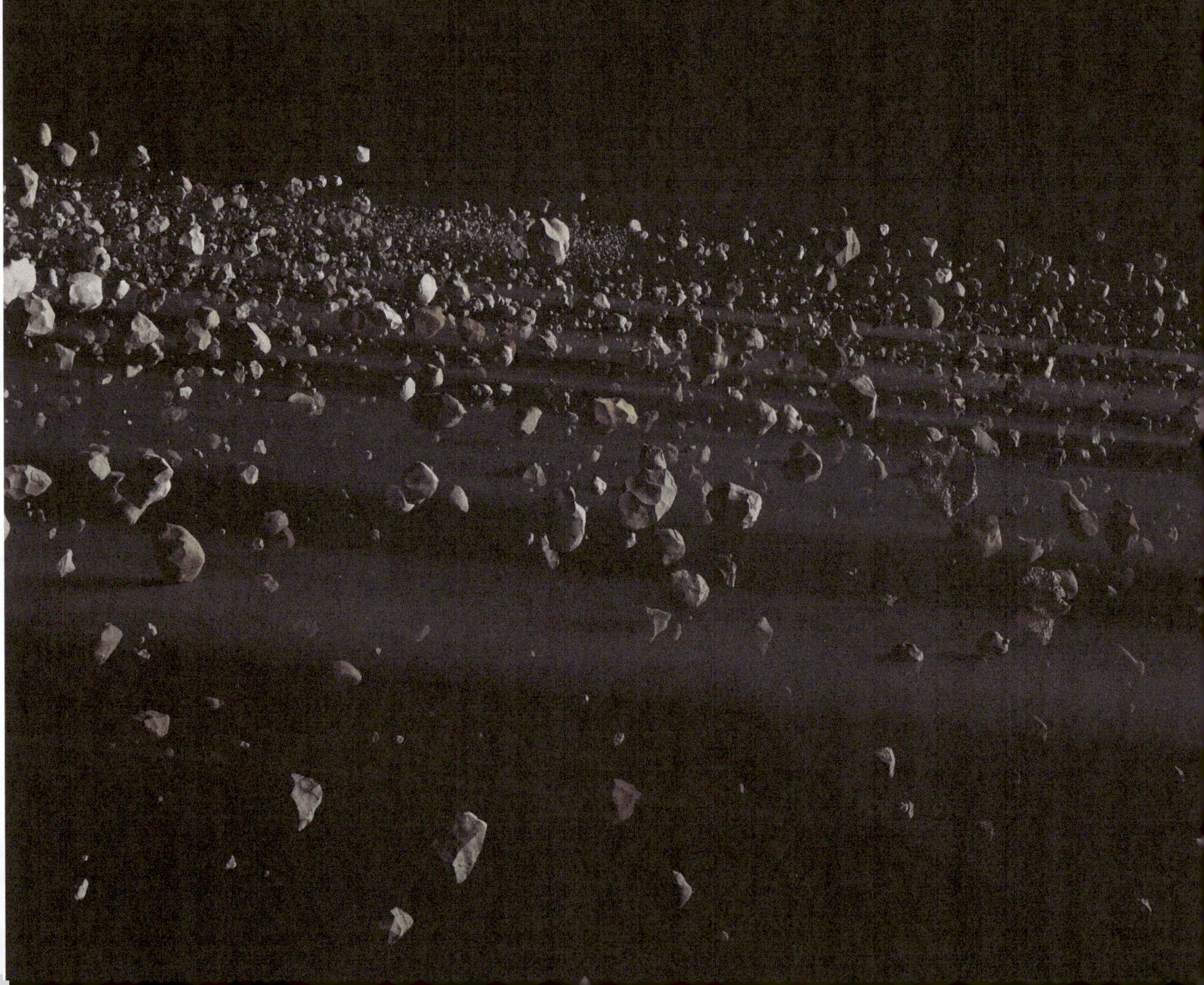

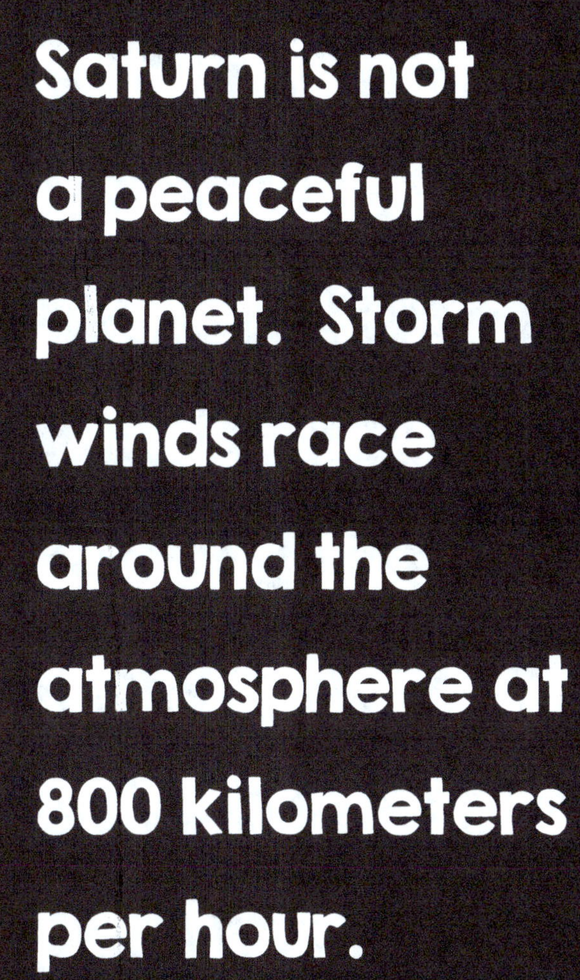

Saturn is not a peaceful planet. Storm winds race around the atmosphere at 800 kilometers per hour.

Saturn's upper atmosphere is divided into bands of clouds.

The average distance between Saturn and the Sun is over 1.4 billion kilometres.

Many of Saturn's moons are named after the Titans.

Saturn takes
29 and a
half years
to make one
complete orbit
of the Sun.

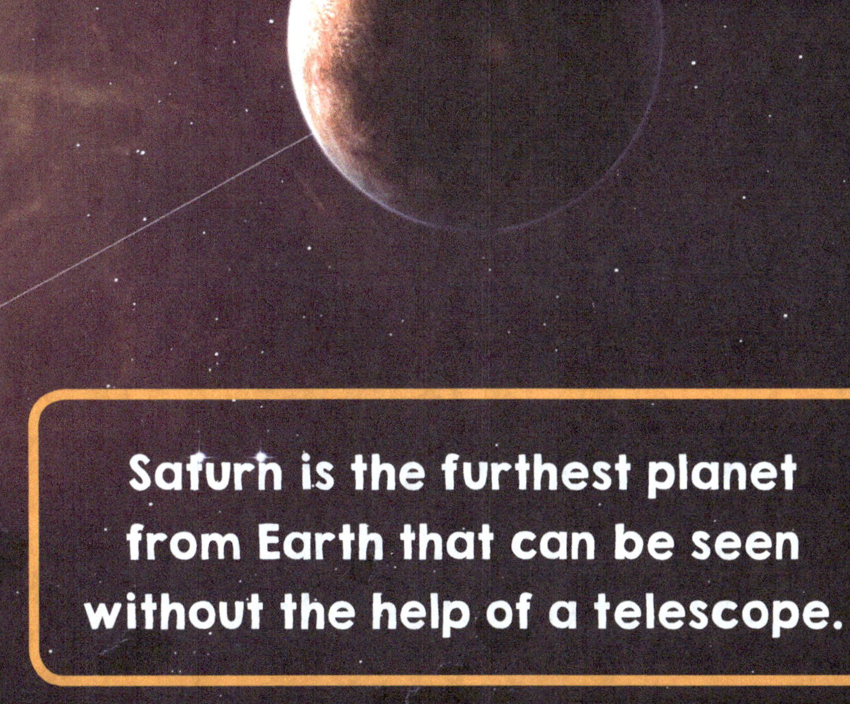

Saturn is the furthest planet from Earth that can be seen without the help of a telescope.

Saturn has
53 official
moons and 9
provisional
moons. This
does not include
the hundreds
of moonlets
comprising
the rings.

Saturn's axis is tilted and as the planet orbits the Sun we get different views of the rings.

Saturn
completes a
full rotation on
its axis in just
over 10 hours.

Galileo originally called Saturn's rings "ears."